DEDICATION

This book is dedicated to everyone who ever lost hope or thought all hope was lost. You are not flying alone, and if you know Jesus Christ as Savior, you have a living hope in Him.

CONTENTS

ACKNOWLEDGMENTS

I want to acknowledge the Lord who gives revelation for everyday living. I also want to acknowledge those who read the manuscript and gave me valuable feedback so that the final product is offered in the excellence you deserve. These folks have encouraged me greatly. I especially want to thank Corinne Miller who edited with skill and precision not only for style, grammar, and readability but kept me accountable doctrinally as well. Thank you all.
And thank God for you.

CHAPTER 1

WHY DO PEOPLE KILL THEMSELVES?

It's important at the outset to realize, and not to trivialize, that everyone at one point or another feels dejected thinking all hope in some way is lost. That hope may be of a relationship, wellness, a dream of some kind. We are all human with very human emotions, even when we come to trust in Christ Jesus. It's also important to note that when we do trust Him with our lives, that all hope is never lost as He is our living hope. But I do not want you to think this book is a bunch of platitudes. I want to be very practical in how the Scriptures apply to every area in our lives. That is why I write books. In this book, however, I am going to specifically address the antidote to thinking all hope is lost and how to regain it — so bear with me.

This is not going to be a very long book. I believe some subject matters require a more direct and practical approach as we need to be able to incorporate them into our daily lives without delay.

Why to people kill themselves? Because they are suffering, and they do not see an end to it. That information somehow becomes unbearable. I answer this question not because I have even struggled in this area or consider myself any level of expert on the matter. However, I am a fellow human, and a very observant one at that. There is only one reason for ending it all and that is because a person becomes overcome with the perception, whether real or imagined, that living is far more difficult that dying.

And while it might be very tempting to consider that person who has chosen the act of ending his or her life as the ultimate act of selfishness, let's be careful to remember that such a person is not thinking rationally about the ramifications of ending it all. Those who elect suicide often consider it the best decision for their families. But I believe that a family's emotional stress will always be outweighed by the pain and suffering that inevitably follows when a loved one takes his or her own life.

It's a tragedy when anyone chooses to end his or her life. But what is especially tragic to me is when a pastor or spiritual leader has chosen to do so. Somehow, I know that it could not have been not an easy decision. I also know that there was nothing natural about it. As such, I am convinced that the level of pressure and spiritual warfare that pastors face is unimaginable to those of us who are not responsible for a flock of believers (and often even other leaders). So many more people than immediate family and friends struggle from such a decision; a whole body of believers and fellow colleagues are astounded and grieved as a result. Many loved ones may take years to recover. And unfortunately, some congregations never recover, and churches may close their doors. No matter how you look at it, when a pastor or spiritual leader commits suicide, nothing is ever the same.

That is my reason for writing this book. As I was reading the Word in 1 Peter, the Lord began to show me the antidote to suicide and suicidal thinking.

Suicide is a subject matter that is somewhat taboo, but it's something we need to discuss as a society and as a Church because it is on the rise for a number of reasons, social and spiritual.

What the Lord showed me is life-changing and life-saving because He is the Giver and Author of life. He has shown that there is indeed another way through to the other side of suffering.

So, let's jump into it.

...

But first, let's pray:

PRAYER OF AGREEMENT & IMPARTATION OF HOPE

Father God, in the name of Jesus and for the sake His people, we ask you to reveal yourself to us afresh and anew as we read and study your Word. Thank you, Lord, for the Living Hope we have in Jesus Christ. Lord, we need a revelation of this Hope to be in and through our beings so that in the evil day we will be able to stand against all the onslaught of the evil one. Lord we know that You are for us and not against us. We also know that You are always with us and that You never leave us nor forsake us. Your promises are yes and amen, and You are not a man that You should lie.

Oh, Lord, we need You as never before. Let Your people draw near to You that You may draw nearer to them and for those who do not yet know You, Father, we pray for ears to hear, hearts to yearn and understand, and wills to choose You before it is too late. Lord, we trust that You will use these few pages to encourage and impart hope and grace to persevere through suffering that in the end we may be able to face You having suffered, and therefore be able to stand ready to receive your glory.

Thank you, Lord, for Your understanding heart. You were tempted in every way we were; that means You also came to a place of despair, the worst despair a person could ever have, yet You persevered and chose the Father's will above Your own. Help us as Your people to do the same that we might not be consumed by evil. Praise you and thank you for answering these prayers. In Jesus' Name. Amen.

CHAPTER 2

WHY DO CHRISTIANS COMMIT SUICIDE?

We know that as believers who are making any level of impact anywhere for Christ against the kingdom of darkness, we are in a war. Make no mistake about that. If you doubt that, then I doubt you truly know the nature of this calling and what you signed up for. It is supernatural even though we live it out in the natural order.

For some reason, suicides by Christians are on the rise. Well, we know the reason — the culmination of time is at hand — the Lord's return is near, and Satan's time as ruler of the world (world system)[i] and of those who have rejected and do not know life in Christ is ending Therefore, the warfare has turned especially ugly. Now we have more Christians than ever, even pastors, committing suicide. It used to be that Christians were giving up their lives due to persecution, but currently, Christians are increasingly *taking* their own lives. What's the answer? What does God have to say about the matter? Well what He has already and always said: Be prepared and use your weapons. For this spiritual warfare, that means spiritual preparations and spiritual weapons. We will delve into more detail with Scripture and the *how to* of the Holy Spirit later.

So, we see that the warfare has turned especially fierce. Christians and even pastors are committing suicide at alarming rates. We cannot be fooled into thinking that the war is limited to only this dimension. A supernatural enemy is on the loose, waging a supernatural warfare against all people. All people you say? Yes, all people. The unbeliever is deceived and, on his way, to making his home with that enemy in eternity, although it does not have to be so. To the unbeliever, he is a danger. Don't forget John 10:10: "The thief comes only to steal, to kill, and to destroy, but I [Jesus Christ], come to give life and it more abundantly." Therefore, as I said before, the answer must be a supernatural one.

You might be wondering why I'm writing a book on suicide, and that would be a fair question. I am doing so because of a Bible reading. Every time I read the Word of God, He shows me something wonderful. As I was reading a Scripture during my devotional time today, I saw what I know to be the antidote to suicide and decided to write this book. Taken with some other key Scripture on spiritual warfare, the Word gives us a most effective arsenal against suicide and suicidal thoughts. And although I have never had such a level of despair as to wanting to end my own life, I have lived through myriad types of spiritual warfare. Am I an expert then? Well, let's say I am experienced and still learning from the Master how to wage that good warfare. I know that we are the victors in this war, yet we know we must live through many battles, all of which we can win if we fight them God's way.

I need to make a point here about a condition we all face: complacency. We tend to relax, but the Bible tells us to be vigilant and sober, not like the five foolish virgins who were unprepared *and* sleeping. At least the others were *prepared* and sleeping. There is no excuse for being unprepared, and neither do we have an excuse for complacency.

As I read in 1 Peter, I found a verse of Scripture that I do believe, once applied along with the other tools which the Lord has given us, is the antidote to suicide and the thoughts that lead to it. But first, let's take a look at the "nature" of spiritual warfare. What is? Paul explains it to us in Ephesians 6. There he tells us what armor to wear to stop the enemy in his tracks or at least stop his weapons — those of both defense and offense — from working against us.

Then we'll look at what Paul tells us about bringing our thought life into alignment with God when it is under attack. These mental strongholds take up residence in the place where thoughts of suicide begin, meaning tactics we need to undertake against the mental strongholds set themselves up to bring us down

We will then focus on the "start verse" that I believe is the antidote to all this struggle with hopelessness and suicidal thinking. This is a good time to remind ourselves that any time we read God's Word, we must also allow the Word to read us and become intimate with us. It is the only *physical* representation of Jesus we still have with us while Holy Spirit is His spiritual representative, leading us into all truth. John 1 calls Jesus the Word Who was in the beginning, then in verse 14 tells us that the Word became flesh. Jesus went back to heaven bodily, but we still have the Word and the Spirit that both bear witness to Him.

When we allow the Word to read us, we are becoming intimate with it, allowing it to become part of us through revelation, so that we can then live it. There is no use in knowing Scripture in your head unless that Scripture has become part of you. It must become flesh in you, too. Thank God that through supernatural means the Word can not only be read, but also lead, teach, and become part of us.

As proof that God's Word is not just words but made to manifest into action, Hebrews 4:12 tells us this:

"For the Word of God is living and powerful, and sharper than any two-edged sword, piercing even to the division of soul and spirit, and of joints and marrow, and is a discerner of the thoughts and intent of the heart."

CHAPTER 3

VICTORY IN THE WARFARE WE FACE

Ephesians 6:10-13

Finally, my brethren, be strong in the Lord and in the power of His might. Put on the whole armor of God, that you may be able to stand against the wiles of the devil. For we do not wrestle against flesh and blood, but against principalities, against powers, against the rulers of the darkness of this age, against spiritual hosts of wickedness in the heavenly places. Therefore, take up the whole armor of God, that you may be able to withstand in the evil day, and having done all,   *to*   *stand.*

****

Here, the Apostle Paul is informing us that as believers our enemies are not the people influenced by the devil but the evil spirits behind evil actions, thoughts, and attitudes. He tells us that we need to be strong the battle. How do we do that? We need to put on our spiritual armor to withstand the spiritual onslaught from the devil. And my friends, suicidal thoughts are most definitely a spiritual onslaught. This armor helps us to be able to stand strong when we are attacked. Again, we need spiritual armor because we face a spiritual enemy. They are not "flesh and blood, but …. principalities, … powers, … [and] rulers of darkness, … spiritual hosts of wickedness in heavenly places." Those heavenly places do not refer to heaven where God lives but to heavenly places as in above us in another dimension.

We must never forget that this spiritual armor to which Paul refers in Ephesians 6 is set up to accomplish and secure victory. These pieces of armor are not toys but effective tools for this type of warfare. Therefore, we must get "dressed" in our armor every day, not just say the words but really put them on. This requires the work of the Holy Spirit in revealing each piece of armor so that we can walk it out. We aim not to just be hearers of the Word but doers also.

So, we are still building on the foundation here. Without a good foundation, we know that any structure built will be faulty and eventually collapse. Our goal is for a solid foundation and a solid "building."

THE ARMOR

Stand therefore, having girded your waist with truth, having

put on the breastplate of righteousness, and having shod your feet with the preparation of the gospel of peace; above all, taking the shield of faith with which, you will be able to quench all the fiery darts of the wicked one. And take the helmet of salvation, and the sword of the Spirit, which is the word of God, praying always with all prayer and supplication in the Spirit, being watchful to this end with all perseverance and supplication for all the saints—[Ephesians 6:14-18]

Belt of Truth

God's truth as revealed constantly by the Holy Spirit keeps us hemmed in and safe from deception. The thought that killing oneself is the only escape from pain and suffering is a huge deception. Let the Holy Spirit minister truth to your inner being as He sets the foundation and protection against the lies of the enemy. The Bible tells us that Satan is the father of lies and all those who are liars. John 8:44: "You are of your father the devil, and the desires of your father you want to do. He was a murderer from the beginning, and does not stand in the truth, because there is no truth in him. When he speaks a lie, he speaks from his own resources, for he is a liar and the father of it."

Notice how the Word addresses lying and murder as attributable to the devil. *"He was a murderer from the beginning and does not stand in truth."* So, we see that murder and deception come from the devil. The idea that there is no hope, a lie, and that the only way out is self-

11

destruction is also a lie from a liar and a murderer. Satan loves to see destruction and he especially delights in the destruction of God's people. To believe his lies is to set oneself up for destruction. The best way is to be hemmed in is to be girded about with the Truth of God.

Everything God says is truth and everything the devil says is a lie even when it sounds like truth. The devil is always seeking to destroy, and Jesus' main goal is to minister life and truth. Jesus is a life-giving Spirit (the second Adam). Just remember, truth and life are attributable to God while death and deception/lies are attributable to the evil one. When you start having thoughts of ending your own life for whatever reason, those are the lies of the enemy seeking to destroy you. Do not listen but immerse yourself in the truth of God.

Here is some truth in which to immerse yourself: Say "I am..."

1. The righteousness of God (Rom. 3:22)

2. The beloved of God (Song of Solomon 2:16, et al)

3. The Bride of Christ (Rev. 21:9, 22:17)

4. Accepted in the beloved (Eph. 1:6))

5. Safe under the wings of the Almighty (Ps. 91:1)

6. Made in the image of God (Gen.1:27)

7. A royal priest (1 Peter 2:9)

8. Part of God's Holy Nation (1 Peter 2:9)

9. Part of His own special people (1 Peter 2:9)

10. Brought out of darkness into (1 Peter 2:9)

11. His marvelous light (1 Peter 2:9))

12. The seed of Abraham (Gal. 3:29)

13. The salt of the earth (Matt. 5:13)

14. The light of the world (Matt. 5:14)

15. A king under the Great King Jesus (Rev. 19:16)

16. Full of the Holy Spirit and Life

17. Equipped with every; thing needed for life and godliness

18. Son/Daughter of the Most High God (Rom. 8:14)

19. Justified by Christ's sacrifice and made innocent as if I had never sinned (Rom. 3:24, 5:1, 8:30; Gal. 2:16)

20. Saved from hell and the grave to have eternal life (John 3:16)

21. Submitted to God (James 4:7)

22. A resister of the devil (James 4:7)

23. Seated in heavenly places (Eph 2:6)

24. Loved by God (John 3:16; 1 John 3:1-2 and through Scripture)

25. Called by God (Rom. 8:30; 1 John 3:1-2)

26. Gifted and given talents by God (Matt. 25:14-30)

27. A minister to the Lord (priest 1Peter 2:9)

28. A minister of God's love to people (Matt.28:19-20)

29. A worshiper of God (John 9:31)

30. One whom God hears (John 9:31)

31. Alive with God for eternity (Rom. 6:11)

32. A visitor to this world until God calls me home or returns (Phil. 3:20)

33. A citizen of heaven (Phil. 3:20)

34. Destined for glory by living through this short time of suffering (1 Peter 5:10; Rom. 8:18; Heb. 2:10)

35. Destined for immortality (2 Cor. 5:1-3)

36. Training for reigning (Matt. 25:21,23)

37. A living epistle of God's love in Christ (2 Cor. 3:2-3)

38. The habitation of Father, Son, and Holy Spirit (John 14:20)

39. Preparing the way for His soon coming return (Matt. 28:19-20)

40. Full of God's living Hope in Christ Jesus (Ps. 39:7;71:5; Col. 1:271 Tim. 1:1; 1 John 3:3)

41. Full of promise (Acts 2:39; Heb.6:17-18)

42. Known by God (2 Tim. 2:19)

43. Unconditionally loved by God (Jer. 31:3; Rom. 8:38-39)

Breastplate of Righteousness

This is the part of the armor that helps us maintain our right standing with God. Notice it covers the heart and vital internal organs. When we think of the physical heart, we recognize that it is the central part of the body determining our life flow in our blood, carrying oxygen to our entire system; the electrical pulse that keeps it going is a mystery of God. The heart is like the engine of our car; without it, the car cannot function. But the breastplate referred to in this passage is metaphorical in that it does not protect the physical heart, but rather the metaphysical or spiritual heart, that is, the central portion of our personal being.

The heart of a person is the central part of the personality of the person or what we call the soul. The soul is who we are on the inside apart from our physical flesh. However, our emotional being is interrelated to our physical being. That is why extreme sadness or stress, or any other negative emotion can and does take a toll on the physical body. So, the heart (soul) is where our mind, will, and emotions are "housed." And again, the health of that part of our being affects everything else. That is where we make decisions. It is where a decision to sin or do a righteous act begins. The heart is what the enemy of our soul attacks because it is the epitome of our soul. It is *where* the battle for the life is fought; indeed, the heart itself is the very thing *over which* it is fought.

You see, when we make decisions, there are consequences for good or bad. For instance, if I am faced with an intense temptation and I fall to it, it's with my heart that I make that decision to sin. Now is that the end of the story? Of course not! At least not as long as I am still breathing. As long as I am still breathing *I have hope*, and Jesus is that Hope. But we will delve more deeply into that in a later chapter when we discuss what I believe to be the actual antidote to suicide. Actually, I believe it is the antidote to what causes us to lose hope in the first place even if the decision made is not to end it all.

So, when we keep that area of our heart protected by keeping our account clean with God, staying humble, repentant, we can protect our emotions from the onslaught of Satan and his minions.

As I said earlier, your mind, will, and emotions are housed in the heart — not the brain. The brain is simply the computer processor that controls how we interact with the world, but it is in your heart that you make decisions. On the other side of a decision to sin is a decision to not sin and to do what is right in the eyes of God, which brings us the benefits of peace with God and blessings from Him.

Similarly, the heart is where we feel emotions such as love, joy, hope, fear, loneliness, and despair. The Bible gives us many pieces of armor to combat anything the enemy would throw at is. A huge reason for people giving up and killing themselves is the emotion of fear, which left unchecked, can graduate into hopelessness and despair and the subsequent decision to harm oneself. In addition, fear left unchecked and unsubmitted to God does invite a demonic spirit, which might be causing the fear in the first place. Here is what you do with it.

Why shoes? I believe that is because believers are charged with taking the Gospel of the Prince of Peace, Jesus Christ, wherever they go. Jesus is the only Way anyone can make peace with God from Whom we became estranged at the Fall of man in the Garden of Eden. Peace is vitally important because a person at peace does not lose hope and plunge into despair. A person of peace knows that trouble is temporary, and that Jesus is the Way and Resolution to all problems. Peace with God prevents us from the need to know everything about our circumstances and the specific outcomes because we know the One Who has it all under control regardless of the end result.

When a person has peace with God, he or she can go into any war-torn area and bring that peace to others, without allowing that warfare to rob him or her of that peace. A person of peace and who has the peace of God does not commit suicide. So, we are to take the peace to others and not let their lack of peace affect us. Jesus said, "Peace I leave with you, My peace I give to you; not as the world gives do I give to you. Let not your heart be troubled, neither let it be afraid."[ii]

These are bold words from Jesus and seemingly impossible, but He starts with the way to maintain that peace by telling us that He has already given it. It is not something a person has to work to receive. He is commanding us to not let our hearts be troubled but have faith in the peace He has already given us. Now let's take a little sidebar. Anything Jesus commands us to do He has already empowered us to do. Further, anything that He has given or promised us, we must appropriate it by faith. To do that, there must be trust in the One promising, belief that what He is promising He is able to provide, and confidence that He is speaking truth. So, it is impossible to have faith in anything Jesus says without believing He is speaking truth, trusting in His ability to provide, and knowing that what He says He will do He will do.

Now if you are one of those people who must control everything — in other words if you don't see it you cannot believe it,— then it is impossible for you to have faith. Yet Jesus (through the writer of Hebrews) tells us that "[W]ithout faith it is impossible to please Him, for he who comes to God *must believe that He is*, and *that He is a rewarder of those who diligently seek Him.*

A person who has active faith in God does not kill himself. There must be a lack of faith, hope, and of peace, albeit temporary. That despair must start growing somewhere where there is a deception that God is not true to His Word and that Jesus set up an impossible standard for us to live by. There must be a temporary lack of belief that Jesus is Who He said He is and could do what He promised to do. Chief among those promises is His promise never to leave us nor forsake us regardless of how we are feeling at the time.

This is why a lifestyle of worship is crucial to our wellbeing as believers. True worship, especially when prophetic in nature, puts us in touch with God no matter how terrible we are feeling, provided we are willing to let Him touch us. But even better than that, when we open our mouths instead of just listen to someone else singing, it is impossible to stay disconnected from God. Impossible! The Bible tells us He inhabits the praises of His people. [Psalm 22:3] So not only is Jesus there through His promise, but He is there truly through our praise. He is always accessible.

That is why, if you are ever hit with thoughts of suicide, hopelessness, and despair, do not delay crying out to Him! This means in worship and in prayer — any way you can — just do it! Of course, seek other help from family and friends; just make sure you are turning to Him first!

Most important: Shield of Faith

This shield if faith is considered the most important piece of the armor. It has the power to "quench the fiery darts" of the devil. In the previous section, I shared quite a bit about faith. Here, in this section, we look at how to actively engage your faith when the devil attacks. When it comes to engaging our faith, the devil, often, if not always, attacks our identity in Christ. Once we have lost our sense of identity, he can more quickly assault and rob us of what is ours. Here is an example of his dirty tricks.

When Jesus had been baptized by his cousin John then driven into the wilderness by the Holy Spirit also with Whom He had just been baptized, one of the tactics the enemy used to try to get Jesus to give up all and to miss His destiny of saving and redeeming mankind was to attack His identity. "If you are the Son of God, ..." [Matthew 4:3,6. Keep in mind Jesus had been fasting; when you are fasting, your body is weaker, but your spirit is stronger. Satan was trying to

19

get Jesus to question His identity as the Son of God. Why? That very position is what demolished Satan's hold over man and that temporary victory he gained at the Fall in the Garden of Eden.

Jesus came to take back what man lost to the devil, and that is why Satan tried so hard to keep things status quo. The stakes could not have been higher. He had to get Jesus to question His position, and thereby, His authority to do what He was about to do… take it all back!

3 Now when the tempter came to Him, he said, "If You are the Son of God, command that these stones become bread."

4 But He answered and said, "It is written, 'Man shall not live by bread alone, but by every word that proceeds from the mouth of God.' "

5 Then the devil took Him up into the holy city, set Him on the pinnacle of the temple, 6 and said to Him, "If You are the Son of God, throw Yourself down. For it is written:

'He shall give His angels charge over you,'

and, 'In their hands they shall bear you up, Lest you dash your foot against a stone.' "

7 Jesus said to him, "It is written again, 'You shall not [a]tempt the LORD your God.' " [Matthew 4:3-7]

So, what do you do when you are bombarded by thoughts of inadequacy and doubt about who and Whose you are? Go back to the Word. Look at all the "I am …" statements on pages 12 through 14 of this book. The Bible has them all. Get your faith renewed by reading God's Word, which also washes and renews your mind. Remind the devil who you are and who he is, a defeated foe. As you are reminding him out loud of who you are and what your inheritance is in Christ, you will be building your faith.

Faith is the one thing the Lord asks if He will find upon His return. [Luke 18:8] Why? Because He knows that our faith will increasingly be tested as His return draws near. But it is easy to re-engage your faith after a temporary crisis. And that is a crucial fact to remember — *all* trouble is temporary because this earth is temporary. The Lord only asks us to trust Him and hold on. Of course, I am not saying that He will bring deliverance only after His glorious return, but rather that all earthly things are temporary. You will also find that in the presence of faith, the enemy will not stick around. He will flee. Many times, he will only flee for a season but in that season as we continue to build our faith, guess what happens when he makes another appearance. Same effect — we engage and exercise our faith and he must flee. But maintaining our sense of identity in who and Whose we are is crucial to winning those battles. We know the war has already been won; however, the battles are fought daily in the natural.

But Hope is alive in Jesus Christ ... *Always!*

Helmet of Salvation

Salvation is the beginning of the story of life in Christ for the believer. Many mistakenly believe it's the culmination, but it is only the beginning. There is a faith walk involved, and the moment of salvation is when that walk starts. Many people begin this life in Christ with an unquenchable zeal for the things of God and a desire to tell everyone about Jesus. One way to describe it is to say that at that time one is "on fire for Jesus." Unfortunately, because we are human, this fire can begin to fade and the trials of life kick in. Now, if the foundation of faith was well built, then the believer can weather any storm, as long as he or she remains *in Christ*. However, we all know that we falter, some of us quite often. Thank God for grace and mercy, which is new every morning. Thank God that He foresaw our struggles and knew that we needed mercy every morning.

Yet, we have been given effective spiritual weapons, or tools, if you will, to remain strong. Again, key to remaining strong is the knowledge that *every struggle is temporary*. And most struggles are happening in the realm of our minds, our thoughts (decisions, plans, processing information, solutions to problems, etc.).

That is why salvation is much like a helmet that protects our thought life from the enemy's schemes. The Bible even tells us what and how to think so that we are not overcome by negative thoughts and emotions, which is many ways, is how Satan sets up camp in our minds.

Philippians 4:6-8 tells us this:

"*Be anxious for nothing,* but in everything *by prayer and supplication with thanksgiving* let your *requests be made known to God.* And the *peace of God,* which passes all understanding, *shall keep your hearts and minds* through Christ Jesus. Finally, brethren, whatsoever things are *true*, whatsoever things are *honest*, whatsoever things are *just*, whatsoever things are *pure*, whatsoever things are *lovely*, whatsoever things are of *good report*; if there be any *virtue*, and if there be any *praise, think on these things.*"

It's interesting to note that we are commanded not to worry. If it were not a choice, it would not be a command. Worry and peace are mutually exclusive. How do we keep from worrying? We do it by letting God in on all our problems and challenges, asking Him for what we need instead of worrying about it. If we lack something, we are to ask Him to provide it; if there is something outside of His will for us, we are to ask Him to remove it. For example, the prophet Jonah did not want to go to Nineveh to preach to the wicked Assyrians, but it was God's will to save the people from destruction; therefore, He did not remove the call to go from Jonah, who finally had to go. [Jonah 1-4]. But regardless of what we are facing, we need to approach God in thankfulness of what He has already done. Then His peace will rest upon us in a way that will cause others to marvel at our response to our trouble.

Then and only then will our hearts and minds be at rest, and all of this is only possible as we remain in Christ. Our peace only exists in Him Who is the Prince of Peace. And being at peace is inconsistent with a desire to harm oneself. After all of the above, we need to guard our minds; then comes the recipe for maintaining our peace in directing our thoughts aright by thinking only these things, which are:

1.True

2. Honest

3. Just

4. Pure

5. Lovely

6. Of good report

7. Virtuous

8.   Praiseworthy

Think of them as "*the 8 of Philippians 4:8.*" And notice they do not only guard your mind but also your heart, your thought life and your emotional life. Think of what that would be worth

as a commodity on the market. Priceless!

So, we are building our arsenal in the war against suicide and suicidal thoughts.

Sword of the Spirit

Most people would end with the last actual piece of armor, the helmet of salvation. Yet Paul goes on with at least four other pieces for setting the armor in place. And isn't it just like God to make this comprehensive! In order to set the armor, we must pray in the Spirit. That means, according to Paul, praying in tongues, your heavenly language. Friends, it is impossible to wage a good warfare in the Spirit without the Holy Spirit Himself. He is the only One who can lead us to victory. This, however, presents a problem for those who do not believe in what Paul encourages us to do in praying and singing with the understanding and with the Spirit.

But we are not done yet.

Praying always in the Spirit

Here, after putting on the armor, prayer in the Spirit sets the armor in place and makes us dangerous and impenetrable to demonic forces.

Being Watchful

This is our reminder that we do not just put our spiritual armor and sit back and relax. We need to be watchful. Why? Because we do not want to wait until the attacker is upon us to start to fight. We need to see the enemy coming so that we can engage the right piece of armor and weapon to be victorious every time. There is nothing worse than a complacent warrior. I know some people would rather see walking out their faith as a walk in the park, smelling the roses; but might I warn you not to do that, at least not just yet? At the same time, we are not to worry and live in fear, but we told that we are soldiers in God's army. We will have eternity to be free of the need to fight the enemy. For now, however, we have a formidable foe, who is also an opportunist.

We need to learn to war as God teaches us. After all, it often takes war, or a readiness to engage in war, to ensure peace. Case in point, King David was the king under whom God chose to unite the people of Israel, yet what was David? He was a warrior. It was only because of his father the warrior securing the peace of Israel, that Solomon, David's son, was able to rule in peace. Yet we see what trouble he got into because he lived in a time of peace. [1 Kings; 2 Samuel; 1 Chron.22]

If we are not watchful, peace can bring about a type of complacency. That is why many Christians of the West who live in the lap of convenience and luxury lack the ability to fight the enemy and his minions with all their schemes. We are living a life that breeds complacency. In addition, many churches avoid discussing spiritual warfare or even the enemy. Of course, we are not to focus on him, but how unwise to ignore his existence! This leaves people susceptible to his devices, chief among these being to get believers to question their faith and in so doing question God.

I am in no way implying that we will not struggle. That would be ridiculous and just plain dishonest. The point is that when we do have trouble, we have already been told what to do, which is what I am laying out in this book. Deal with your problems Biblically by engaging God. Should you engage a psychiatrist? That is up to you. But make sure He is your main Counselor and that your psychiatrist is of like faith. You do not want to engage tactics that would make things worse.

Persevering and praying for other saints

I love this! Isn't just like God to say with this mandate: "I know you have your own troubles but don't forget to pray for your brothers and sisters in the faith who are also struggling in some way"! By the way, there is no chapter and verse for that. I just see that as God encouraging us to stay connected and loving the Body as we go through our own challenges as he commands so often through the Scriptures. [Gal. 6:2].In addition, how many times have you cared for, shared with, or gone out of your way to help another when you had a need yourself only to see God take care of your need without your direct involvement? God loves a cheerful and sacrificial giver. [2 Cor. 9:6-7]. When that sacrifice is made for His Kingdom, He goes to lengths to get answers for His children.

This means that we are not to isolate ourselves from the Body of Christ when we are faced with trials. That is a direct tactic of the enemy — to isolate and destroy. It makes sense that if you are in a healthy giving and taking relationship in which you and at least one or two other people share their lives, everyone involved is less likely to give up hope and give into despair.

PRAYER FROM OPENING SCRIPTURE

Dear Lord, help me to be strong in the power of Your might. I put on Your whole armor, so that I may be able to stand against the wiles of the devil. I realize that we do not wrestle against flesh and blood, but against principalities, against powers, against the rulers of the darkness of this age, against spiritual hosts of wickedness in the heavenly places. I, therefore, take up the Your whole armor, that I may be able to withstand in the evil day, and having done all, to stand. Father, I also realize that wrestle is only for a limited time and as I remain in you, I will overcome the evil one in due time. Thank you, Lord for victory in Jesus. Amen.

CHAPTER 4

VICTORY OVER THE ATTACK ON OUR MINDS

2 Cor 10:3-6

For though we walk in the flesh, we do not war according to the flesh. For the weapons of our warfare are not carnal but mighty in God for pulling down strongholds, casting down arguments and every high thing that exalts itself against the knowledge of God, bringing every thought into captivity to the obedience of Christ, and being ready to punish all disobedience when your obedience is fulfilled.

****

Keep in mind that the enemy has been keeping tabs on each of us all of our lives. He has been listening to and watching us. That is not to put you in fear but to help you to understand that we have an observant enemy who, while he is not omniscient. is indeed quite knowledgeable. In other words, he knows how and where to attack us in our minds. We all have varying weaknesses and he is aware of them. We all have (or had) varying wounds, and he is aware of them. That does not, however, mean that he has to win the battle. We have tools with which the Lord has provided us — many of them. The strongest one is that He has already won the victory over the enemy. We simply need to agree with this in word and action. Don't proclaim something in agreement with God and do the opposite. When you do that, you lose credibility with God and man, and you also lose authority and effectiveness in fighting against the wiles of the enemy, Satan.

Most people know and believe that as humans we are three-part, otherwise known as triune, beings. We are a spirit, soul, and body. Our spirit and our soul are eternal while our current body is temporary. We will one day get a more permanent model but for now, this body is temporary and in decay. This may seem a little morbid, but it's true. So, we are indeed made up of temporary flesh for now. Our individual spirits, that is my spirit and your spirit, once redeemed by Christ through our decision, always says, "yes" to God's will and way. That's why we have the saying, the "spirit is willing by the flesh is weak." Our soul however, is part of our fallen being, and as we submit to God, it is being transformed to the likeness of Christ, Who always said "yes' to God, spirit, soul, *and* body (even to death on a cross).

Yet, because we are primarily eternal, our weapons for the war that is being waged against us are not typical or even physical weapons. Therefore, when the enemy comes against us with a barrage of negative thoughts, we need to fight him with spiritual, not physical, weaponry. And by the way, the carnal advice of people does not equate to spiritual weapons. The spiritual weapons to which Paul refers as the armor (which as we have already discussed) require a close and personal relationship to Christ as they need to be used in faith. Only by submitting to Christ are the weapons of any use. Remember the sons of Sceva who tried to battle the devil without a relationship to Jesus? They received a thorough thrashing because they had no position from which to wage that warfare. Simply put, they could not use the name of One Whom they did not know. [Acts 19:11-20]

So, what does this all mean? Well, it means you do not just stumble upon victory over Satan. Remember, the enemy has an organized network of "spiritual" beings, who can at times manifest into the spirit, waging war against God's people. You see, even though the war in heaven was already fought and won by Almighty God, the enemy is still waging a losing war, and he does gain a battle here and there. Those battles are gains because we fail to wage a good warfare. And waging warfare is first done in prayer. Without prayer, there is no victory for the believer. This is a good time to go back to the spiritual armor of Ephesians 6 and the follow-up steps from Paul. We must pray, in the Spirit and with the understanding! Always!

I introduced this chapter with 2 Corinthians 10, which refers to "casting down every high thing that exalts itself against belief in God." It is important to note that is a personal "high thing." It refers to something that causes you, though perhaps not consciously, to replace and substitute your faith in God with faith in something or someone else. Common substitutes are competing belief systems, money, a relationship, an activity, a habit. You name it. The Bible tells us that these things are to be cast down; really, it's advocating violence against anything that would make you question Christ or hamper your faith in Him. Often, it's the perceived size of a problem that causes the fear and not the likely outcomes. Fear itself causes us to think unreasonably in often anticipating unrealistic outcomes. You name it, it can be a stronghold. And where is that stronghold? In the mind, where most of spiritual warfare is waged.

Remember this: God knows exactly how you feel because the Son of God has experienced everything we have. Yet, we are the ones who have to cast down the strongholds with the tools and weapons He has given us for protection. Even if an infiltration is made because we failed to use the defensive weaponry He has provided to us, we do have the offensive ones — primarily the Word of God, which is our Sword of the Spirit. God's Word provides an invincible weapon against which the enemy has no power when it proceeds from the mouth of a Spirit-emboldened born-again blood-washed saint of the Most High. Yes! That is who you are; and if you are not sure, call me or write me through the Facebook page for this book.

****

PRAYER FROM OPENING SCRIPTURE

"Lord, I know that although I am made of flesh that I am not to wage a fleshly war against the enemy. I know that the weapons you have provided for my victory are not carnal and visible, yet they are mighty in You to pull down the strongholds built up in my mind and being that have been against my knowledge and faith in you. I am casting down any argument and high thing that attempts to disarm my mind of the truth about You, Your love for me, and Your will for my life. Lord, I am bringing all these things captive in obedience to You and I am ready to punish all disobedience after my obedience is complete. I pray all of this in the name of Jesus Christ. Amen."

Your prayer does not have to be exactly as laid out here, but it should cover all the components of the Scripture with sincerity. God will help you as you do your part.

PART II

THE ANTIDOTE TO SUICIDE AND

SUICIDAL THOUGHTS

CHAPTER 5

THE ANTIDOTE TO SUICIDE AND

SUICIDAL THOUGHTS:

HOPE THROUGH HIS RESURRECTION

1 Peter 1:3-5

Blessed be the God and Father of our Lord Jesus Christ, who according to His abundant mercy has begotten us again to a living hope through the resurrection of Jesus Christ from the dead, to an inheritance incorruptible and undefiled and that does not fade away, reserved in heaven for you, who are kept by the power of God through faith for salvation ready to be revealed in the last time.

****

Well, we have finally arrived at the antidote for which we have been aiming all along. However, without the foundation we have just set, there would be nothing to build upon to fight the intensified war raging against mankind and especially against the children of God. It is heartbreaking to hear of a Christian committing suicide, but so much worse to hear of a pastor or other Christian leader with followers committing suicide. In many ways, it is unimaginable.

But please, I ask you, do not get me wrong, I *know* the war is fierce. I have faced it, though in a different way than we are addressing here; but it has been fierce nonetheless. I do not believe there is one prophetic person who has not faced significant resistance and warfare, both inside and outside of the body of believers. To be clear, I do not believe the true Church of God fights God's mouthpieces and therefore, His agenda. However, those with *another* agenda do. So, we all face warfare; that's not unusual. It is how we respond to that warfare that differentiates the overcomer from the one who has been overcome.

Let's examine the Scripture passage at the beginning of this chapter, piece by piece, to get to the antidote that I believe the Lord has set up for us to maintain or regain hope, avoid or get out of despair, and to never give up on God.

According to His abundant mercy has begotten us again

The Bible tells us that through God's abundant mercy He has begotten us *again*. This means that He had already begotten us but then we were lost. In other words, He had us and then He didn't. The interrupting factor, you may already have guessed, was the fall of mankind in the Garden of Eden. God made man, then man chose to separate from God through sin. Without a redeeming factor, man would be lost forever. So, through Christ, God delivers from that lost condition those who choose to be "begotten again." Once redeemed, we are set to live with God for eternity and we do not have to die until He calls us home. God never intended for man to determine the time of his own death. That is a decision reserved for the One Who gave us life in the first place.

Living hope through the resurrection of Jesus Christ

This is a crucial portion of this passage of Scripture. Without Jesus Christ, there is no hope in this life or in the one to come. But notice, this is a "living hope," and it was secured by nothing other than Christ's resurrection from the dead. Notice, without His resurrection, we would have no hope. All of mankind would remain in the lost and condemned state we entered by the Fall. So even though the fall into sin was man's fault, God, through Christ, took the blame on Himself, died and was resurrected, causing that original hope of eternal life, initially given to man, to be reinstated. The word "redeemed" has two meanings: the first one is "to compensate for the faults of bad aspects of something," or it can mean to "regain possession of something you once had through the exchange of payment." Here, both meanings apply, but the second is the most applicable to man's condition. Jesus was buying us back for His Father by His death and resurrection. Someone had to take the blame and die for the sin of all mankind, and that person had to be perfect and undeserving of that death.

Through Christ's resurrection He bought us that living hope, and no one with this living hope has to die prematurely and certainly not at his or her own hand. Jesus died so that no one else has to be condemned to death for their sin against God.

Inheritance incorruptible and undefiled and that does not fade away

Anything that we can see in this natural realm is fading away because it is all corruptible. Even our physical bodies, this flesh, is fading away and, sad to say, decaying. That is until we are given an incorruptible body. Therefore, the same is true with regard to this inheritance we have through Christ. It is incorruptible and undefiled because it is not of this earthly realm. It is kept in heaven as explained below. It cannot fade and cannot be corrupted or defiled.

Reserved in heaven for you

There are some things we cannot have or experience here on earth. This natural realm, as we are taught so often in the Bible, is at best temporary. Everything now existing in this natural realm, except eternal mankind, will be burned up. God will make a new incorruptible earth to replace this corrupted one. He will also make a new heaven, and there we will live with Him forever. [Rev.21:1].

Therefore, it is impossible to live your "best" life now in this dispensation or realm. The best things are eternal, currently invisible, and without price. Anyone can see that most people are not living their best lives. This world is a mess with much suffering and evil. No, it will not always be so because God is merciful. It is because of this two-fold mercy that He is waiting to send Jesus back to receive His own. First, He is waiting for everyone to get the Good News of His love and plan for them. Second, He will not extend that time lest men completely destroy each other or the planet.

Jesus will return at just the right time, and we need to get ourselves and others ready. No one should take the risk of missing the fulfillment of his or her reward here on earth by ending his or her own life and in so doing miss the full reward which Jesus is bringing back with Him. The temporary pain we must endure in this world is worth the eternal reward He is bringing with Him.[iii]

Kept by the power of God through faith for salvation

This says a mouthful! The reward or inheritance, which God has been keeping for us in heaven far from the elements which corrupt, is kept by His power through our saving faith. Your faith for salvation, or your entire being, is connected to the power God exerts to keep your reward and inheritance for you. Friend, that means that we must persevere to the end. There must be no giving up early and opting out of life. We cannot opt out once we opt in. When I say, we *cannot*, I mean we certainly have a choice; but I own urge you, do not opt out. God has you and by His power will keep you if you do not give up. Please hear me! Do not give up! God has you!

PRAYER FROM OPENING SCRIPTURE

Dear God, thank you for your abundant mercy through which we have received a living hope through the resurrection of Jesus Christ Who died for us. His resurrection means by accepting His death on the Cross, I have already died, and now I have also resurrected with Him Thank you for the inheritance that I have through Christ, that is incorruptible and, therefore, eternal and undefiled and, therefore, pure. That means my inheritance is perfect and it cannot fade away. It is reserved in heaven for me when you choose to call me home to be with You forever. In the meantime, Lord, I thank you for keeping my inheritance, by Your power through my faith for salvation in Jesus Christ, that is ready to be revealed in the last days. Lord. I give you praise, and honor for Jesus and it is in His name I pray. Amen.

CHAPTER 6

THE ANTIDOTE TO SUICIDE AND

SUICIDAL THOUGHTS:

SUFFERING THAT TESTS OUR FAITH

1 Peter 1:6-9

In this you greatly rejoice, though now for a little while, if need be, you have been grieved by various trials, that the genuineness of your faith, being much more precious than gold that perishes, though it is tested by fire, may be found to praise, honor, and glory at the revelation of Jesus Christ, whom having not seen you love. Though now you do not see Him, yet believing, you rejoice with joy inexpressible and full of glory, receiving the end of your faith—the salvation of your souls.

****

We must never forget how Jesus suffered. The Bible tells us that His suffering taught Him obedience. Imagine that! The Son of God had to suffer, and that taught Him obedience. Hebrew 5:8 says,

"[T]hough He was a Son, *yet* He learned obedience by the things which He suffered."

Since the student cannot be greater that the Teacher, and we follow in His footsteps, so too must we suffer in this fallen world. That is but for a short time. Yet, we too, learn to obey and trust Him even when we suffer greatly. Jesus only received glory once He had suffered. So too, are we glorified when we suffer for Him. This is not the message that will fill churches and sell CDs, but it is directly from the Bible. And it is the wisdom of God to train us this way instead of through constant comfort and fineries. What soldier learned to fight sitting on a couch eating potato chips? Life can be hard, and He knows that because He lived it when He walked the earth.

Do we suffer because God likes to see people suffer? No, far from it. We suffer because of the dispensation in which we live. In other words, we suffer because that is the state of the world since the fall of mankind. It's the reason God had to destroy the earth during Noah's time. Without me going into a whole theological discourse, suffice it to say that the Bible tells us that fallen angels had mixed with humans and produced a race by which there was much evil in the world in addition to man's own evil. [Gen. 6:1-4]. The races had to be destroyed, as there was no redemption possible to anyone unless that which was utterly polluted be eliminated. Now, while that does not explain why we as individuals must suffer, it still goes back to Fall.

Suffering begets suffering which begets more suffering, right? Not so fast. You see, a Divine Interrupter was born. His name was and is Jesus Christ. Post-Noah, our Hope has a name. Yes, there is suffering still; but the resolution is sure, and the time is temporary. Jesus has made a way, actually, "He *is* the way, the truth, and the life, and no one comes to the Father except through Him." [John 14:6] That is, no one can enter into a relationship with God but through Jesus — because He became one of us. Because He was born, suffered, and was glorified, that is also our lot. We too suffer. But the difference is that because He suffered, died, and rose again to life, that is He overcame death, we can too. He tells us in John 16:33 that in this world we will suffer but that He has overcome the world. You see the only way to outlast a temporary season of suffering is by remaining in Him. We suffer, but the Divine Interrupter overcame so that we could, too.

In this you greatly rejoice, though now for a little while, if need be, you have been grieved by various trials, that the genuineness of your faith, being much more precious than gold that perishes, though it is tested by fire...

We are told to "greatly rejoice." In what? We rejoice in the incorruptible undefiled reward God is storing up for us in heaven! We do not want to be disqualified from receiving our rewards.[iv] In 1 Corinthians 9:27, the apostle Paul writes of preaching about the goodness of God, His redemption, and the inheritance and rewards awaiting us in heaven, then being disqualified from receiving this same prize he preached about. What a powerful description of doing something, like giving up on life, then not qualifying for the prize you told others about.

Peter tells us here — and Christ had warned us about trials and tribulations — that there will be times when we will be grieved by all kinds of trials. Yet, we see here that our trials are not in vain; they come to test our faith to see whether it is genuine. He tells us that our faith — now hear this — is more precious than gold because even precious gold eventually perishes. Even gold, as precious and durable as it is, is not eternal. It is still temporal and will hold up for a time according to its level of purity, even when subjected to fire.

Isn't that just like a trial, often called "trial by fire?" Trials test our mettle and what we are made of. Just like that gold, how precious and how sustainable and sustaining is our faith. If that faith is in Jesus Christ, and we maintain it by hearing the Word of God, then it will stand up to the hottest fire, the greatest pressure, and the longest time. That is not to say that any of it is easy; yet, Jesus did say His "burden is light, and His yoke is easy." [Matthew 11:30] Are you carrying His burden or your own? A burden he had not given you or a yoke He has not put on you will indeed overcome you. Yet, to walk with Him and in right relationship to Him through whatever you are experiencing will result in your walking in the power of an overcomer.

Don't succumb to the trials and pressures of life instead of depending on and drawing near to Christ. He is there to deal with whatever has come against you from wherever it has come.

[M]ay be found to praise, honor, and glory at the revelation of Jesus Christ, ⁸ whom having not seen you love. Though now you do not see Him, yet believing, you rejoice with joy inexpressible and full of glory...

As we persevere through trials, in pursuit of Christ and captured by His love for us, He is revealed in us. In this way, He is praised, honored, and glorified though we have not seen him in person, flesh to flesh. We may not see Him with our physical eyes, but we do behold Him in our hearts with the eyes of our hearts. By His Spirit we see Him, and with that comes a joy that in unexplainable and inexpressible and full of His glory. [1 Peter 1:8]

Isn't it astounding that all of that can come out of suffering our temporary trials? It goes to show that it's not just what we go through that makes us, it's the nature of God that comes through us when we do. Will we endure in joy, or will we whine and complain to people about our difficulties? I am learning that we need to take our trials to God. He can handle our honest brokenness of heart; but pity parties we throw, or the ones thrown for us by our friends, He does not condone and certainly does not bless.

Now, that is not in response to people experiencing real devastation; but when the enemy convinces us to indulge self-pity, that usually does not end well. His desire is to get us to doubt God and the fact that He is good and means us good. That is why we have 2 Corinthians 10 teaching us about the weapons of our warfare. We must understand that.

[R]eceiving the end of your faith — the salvation of your souls.

Our completed salvation has not happened yet. Our *spirits* were saved when we decided to follow Christ. Our *souls*, however, are going through this lifelong transformation as we commit and submit more and more to Christ. Our *bodies* will be the last to be saved as the ones we have now are only temporary. At Christ's return we will be as He is now, with an incorruptible and undefiled body. It is interesting that we focus on the temporary part of our being more than anything else with hardly any regard for the eternal. The spirit and soul part are imperishable, so they're not going anywhere.

As we await the complete salvation of our souls, we trust God through the Holy Spirit to continue to transform us in the image of His Son, Jesus Christ.

Let Jesus have His way. He is not done with you yet. Trials and all, He will use it all to His glory and for your good.

Don't give up on Him and don't give up on yourself.

PRAYER FROM OPENING SCRIPTURE

Dear Lord, thank you for the joy that I have access to in You at all times. In You I can greatly rejoice, though now for a little while, because I live in this world I experience suffering. Yes, I have been grieved by various trials, but that's only so that the genuineness of my faith is being tested by the fires of this affliction. I know that my faith is so much more precious than gold that eventually becomes corrupted and perishes, even though it has been tested by fire. I pray that I may be found to praise, honor, and glory at the revelation of Jesus Christ, whom having not seen I truly love. Though now it hard to see Him in all of this, yet I believe, and I rejoice with joy inexpressible and full of Your glory. And in the end, I will have what I have been waiting for in faith — the full salvation of my soul.

CHAPTER 7

THE ANTIDOTE TO SUICIDE AND

SUICIDAL THOUGHTS:

THE MIND, OUR THOUGHTS & OUR OBEDIENCE

1 Peter 1:13-16

Therefore gird up the loins of your mind, be sober, and rest your hope fully upon the grace that is to be brought to you at the revelation of Jesus Christ; [14] as obedient children, not conforming yourselves to the former lusts, as in your ignorance; but as He who called you is holy, you also be holy in all your conduct, because it is written, "Be holy, for I am holy."

****

Therefore, gird up the loins of your mind, be sober,

It's important to notice the progression of the antidote to suicide and suicidal thoughts. None of this has anything to do with external appearance; all of it is going on internally. That means we cannot always know who is suffering in this way. When asked how we're doing, it's customary to say, "fine" or to just focus on the good things in our lives. Very few people will give you the truth. Society encourages us to focus on the positive and ignore — certainly not to speak — of those things which are negative.

But here, we are encouraged by the Lord through the Apostle Peter to pay attention to and actively protect our minds from the onslaught of the enemy. He is saying gird up your loins, cover and protect the sensitive parts of your mind. Notice, loins are also what produce the fruit of the body, that is, the sexual organs of a man. Similarly, our mind is where the fruit of our existence is conceived. While the brain is where our central nervous system is housed, our minds are where the central part of our soul is found. Therefore, it makes sense that the enemy or our souls would attack the central part of our souls.

The mind, the will, and the emotions are inexorably linked together in the soul. It's easy to see the connection between the mind and the will. We think to do a thing and by our will we do it. But in between are our emotions, and depending on the personality, the emotions may play a central role in what the person decides to do. Some people act out of pure impulse; some are impulse shoppers. In addition, an event might feed into an impulsive act even for a very prudent person. That event could be receiving good news, winning something, or receiving very bad news. As humans, we are all subject to acting impulsively. That is what this portion of the Scripture is addressing. Being settled in one's mind safeguards us from impulsiveness.

As an aside, why do you think there are all these products at the cash register in the store? Those products, such as magazines, chocolate or other candy, gum, sodas, are the ones that appeal to impulse shoppers. Usually, if it's at the cash register, you most likely do not need it, or it may be downright bad for you.

and rest your hope fully upon the grace that is to be

brought to you at the revelation of Jesus Christ;

After girding up the loins of our minds, we are encouraged to rest our hope fully on the grace as Christ is revealed in us. Do you remember when Jesus told the disciples to cross over to the other side and such a storm rose up that they thought they were all going to die? [Mark 4:35; Mark 5:21; Luke 8:22] What was Jesus doing in all that turbulence? He was fast asleep in the back of the boat. He was certainly not worried about the storm or about getting to the other side safely. Do you think He was unaware of what was happening? Certainly, not!

Similarly, when storms arise in our own lives, we can do the same as did Christ, resting securely in the Father, His Source of everything. We must protect our minds in our areas of weakness.

Essentially, we need to be ready for an attack because it will come. But then, we must rest in Christ. Christ as revealed in us ministers not only to us but through us to those in our environment who are reading us as *letters* from God.

By showing our peace in the storm and speaking peace to our atmosphere when moved to by the Holy Spirit, we show others the ways of the Kingdom, that as children of the King, we are not swayed by every wind and storm. Our hope rests on the sure foundation of Christ. That is the revelation of Jesus Christ that the world is looking for. Who is the Revealer of Jesus Christ? He is the Holy Spirit, that third member of the Trinity. The Father and the Holy Spirit both point to the Son.[v]

[A]s obedient children, not conforming yourselves to the former lusts, as in your ignorance; ¹⁵ but as He who called you is holy, you also be holy in all your conduct, ¹⁶ because it is written, "Be holy, for I am holy."

It's vitally important to live in a place of obedience to God. That has to be the greatest protector against the wiles of the devil and our foundation for exercising our authority in Christ. Without that foundation, none of the other weapons of our warfare will properly work because we are not in right standing with God. But when we are in right standing with God, no devil in hell can stop us. Now, let's remember that it's not the sin that angers God so much as the refusal to repent of everything from pride to lying. By this, I mean some people sin in ignorance. I won't bother to include a list here. Chances are you know when you are in sin; if you don't, then you are still in need of salvation. But at salvation, the Holy Spirit comes to teach and train us to be like Jesus Christ, and part of that training is being convicting when we are getting off track.

Some people despise warnings. I don't understand those people. Love warns — end of story. If you tell me that you don't like it when people warn you about sin or try to teach you how to live a Godly life, then I will tell you that you don't like peace, safety, and living the life God has prepared for you. And truly, that is up to you; but it also makes you appear insane. God sent His only Son, Jesus Christ, to die on a cursed cross for your sin and mine. The least we could do is to follow His counsel for success. That is what the Bible is. It contains examples of people, just like you and me, who lived before us and were in many respects just like us. They fell, they sinned, they doubted, they thought their tasks were impossible, and cited all the other excuses we offer God as to why what we are facing now is just too much.

We are not only to be obedient to Christ but also non-conforming to this world system and all the lusts involved in it. We are specially to avoid our former areas of lust and weaknesses where temptation may cause us to fall into sin. For instance, if you were a former alcoholic, it would be unwise to still meet with friends at the bar you used to frequent, or any bar, for that matter.

The verse also mentions that we were once ignorant to our sin and our need to obey God; but now, we no longer have that excuse. We were once steeped in our former worldly lusts, for which God has forgiven us. But now, we have a calling to be holy *in our conduct* as He who called us is holy. The words "in our conduct" disprove the common argument that holiness is only an internal state of being and requiring matching behavior is, as some call it, legalistic. Well, it can only be called legalistic if you can call God legalistic. He requires what He requires. We do not get to be God's judges. He does not run His Kingdom by committee.

His will must be done in our lives so that we can be doers of His Word and not just hearers only. He says, "but **as** He who called you *is* holy, you also be holy in all *your* conduct..." [1 Peter 1:15]

That means, as Peter has been encouraging us here, we are girding up our minds, being obedient and non-conforming to the world and its lusts, staying on the side of holiness. And as for operating in holiness, we cannot do this by ourselves. By the way, in case I have failed to sufficiently emphasize it, we cannot do any of this by ourselves; we must have the help of the Holy Spirit. That is imperative.

PRAYER FROM OPENING SCRIPTURE

Lord, because of Who you are and my place in You and as a victor in this earthly battle doing my part to stand and face the evil one, *dressed* in You I gird up the loins of my mind because that is where the battle is being waged against me. And as I remain sober, I can rest my hope fully upon the grace that is to be brought to me at the revelation of the Lord Jesus Christ. I commit to be Your obedient child, not conforming myself to the former lusts that plagued me, as in my ignorance; but as He who called me is holy, I will also be holy in all my conduct because it is written, "Be holy, for I am holy." Thank you, Lord that it is done. In Jesus' Name. Amen.

CHAPTER 8

THE ANTIDOTE TO SUICIDE AND

SUICIDAL THOUGHTS:

REDEMPTION THROUGH THE BLOOD OF CHRIST

1 Peter 1:17-19

And if you call on the Father, who without partiality judges according to each one's work, conduct yourselves throughout the time of your stay here in fear; [18] knowing that you were not redeemed with corruptible things, like silver or gold, from your aimless conduct received by tradition from your fathers, [19] but with the precious blood of Christ, as of a lamb without blemish and without spot.

****

And if you call on the Father, who without partiality judges according to each one's work, conduct yourselves throughout the time of your stay here in fear;

While we do not focus on works or believe in a works-for-salvation doctrine — that is unbiblical — our works are indeed important. James says that "faith without works is dead." (James 2:20) Faith in Christ leads us to do works in His Name, so works are important. We are workers in His vineyard, but apart from the Vine, Jesus Christ, we can do nothing[vi]. So here we see that God, the Father, will mete out rewards according to our works while here on earth. So, Peter here is exhorting us to let our conduct align with that fact. With that in mind, there is to be a holy reverential fear while we are here on earth.

Why is this important? Well, even our human sense of justice is based on a merit system. A person serves the time prescribed according to the crime he committed, while the Olympian receives the medal based on his performance in his event. If it were not so, the world would be even more chaotic than is appears now. Believe it or not, because of the presence of the Holy Spirit on earth, we are one Person away from absolute bedlam here on earth. Without Him, a relatively good life on earth would be impossible. Unfortunately, that day is fast approaching.

With that in mind, what is to be our posture? It is to be one of faith that we, as believers, old and new, or pre-believers veering towards trust in God, have a sense of God's ability to help us through anything. We can stand firm in faith that nothing is impossible for Him.[vii]

Let's not let fear have any kind of dominion over our lives. God has not given us that spirit, He has instead given us *power, love. and sound mind.*[viii] This means that fear brings with it powerlessness, lovelessness, and insanity. If a person remains in fear for long enough, this is his lot. Please understand I am not speaking of a fight-or-flight kind of fear or the momentary fear that causes you to quickly move out of the way of an oncoming car. That is a defense mechanism designed by God for our preservation. No, the fear I am referring to here is one that is terrifying and often paralyzing. Usually, with that type of fear, the thing feared will rarely, if ever, happen. And even if it happens, there is a solution that does not require drastic action such as self-inflicted wounds. Those who trust God also trust that He knows what we are facing and that *He has already prepared the way of escape and resolution.* [1 Corinthians 10:13]

knowing that you were not redeemed with corruptible things, like silver or gold, from your aimless conduct received by tradition from your fathers,

Those words recognize that an eternal problem required an eternal solution, and that an eternal once-and-for-all redemption would require an incomparable and unique sacrifice. Gold, though precious and durable through time, will eventually become corrupted, and even more so silver. This Scripture is telling us that the traditions of men, no matter how well meaning, could never save us. There needed to be another way by which God could regain and buy back

His family. And since He would be the One this Sacrifice was to appease and satisfy, He would have to not only set the standard, but provide it. Sinful man had tried but could only do so for a year at a time with the annual sacrifice in the temple. [Exodus 30:10] This and other traditions of men were insufficient. These were corruptible things that could never completely fulfill the requirement. So, God would supply His own sacrificial Lamb.

3

but with the precious blood of Christ, as of a lamb without blemish and without spot.

The only acceptable Sacrifice that could eternally redeem the family that God "lost" in the Garden of Eden was a perfect, spotless, and sinless one. Further, since, it was man himself that needed redemption, the life of a Man would be required for the blood sacrifice. But what man could pass the test? A sinful man could never die for the sins of all; he would have already sinned. The only other man who was ever sinless was pre-Fall Adam. No, the only One who could be a sinless Man had to be God Himself, and He would have to step into time and into the creation He made. Astoundingly, God would have to become like the creature He made and die to regain the creature's eternal status. This is a mystery to us, but suffice it to say, the blood of Jesus, Who was tempted as we are yet remained sinless in complete submission to His Father, was the only acceptable sacrifice. Jesus, Son of God, would step into an earthly body to become the Son of Man.

What does this have to do with suicide and suicidal thoughts? This entire book so far has sought to demonstrate our value to God. God Who is perfect in every way, did not *need* man but wanted fellowship with beings that were like Him, and so made us to look and act like Him. He made a family. You are made in the image of God and nothing and no one can take that away from you. He is faithful and available to help in any situation. Try Him! Reach out to Him in prayer (talk to Him honestly about anything, especially those pressing challenges that are leading to thoughts of suicide). See if God does not step into your situation. He may come to you by ministering through one of His sons or daughters, or in some other way; but a genuine heart-felt cry to Him will always be answered.

PRAYER FROM OPENING SCRIPTURE

Father in heaven, thank You for Your love and Your Sacrifice of sending Your Son Jesus to die the death of a criminal so that we can have eternal life with You. Help me with my thoughts, Lord. I give all my burdens to You and trust that You will show me the way to solve these problems. If my problems are in my thought life, Lord, I give You all these ways of thinking that make me want to do harm to myself. God, I trust You and right now, I focus on You, worship, and praise You for delivering me from these ways of thinking and bringing me to sit with Jesus in heavenly places. There is no sin, no sadness, and no warfare of the mind or anything of that nature in heaven. Therefore, I have risen above this fray and will remain with You in Spirit until the day that You bring me to You at Your appointed time. Teach me the lessons I am to take away from this season, and make me into the person of Jesus, that I may help those people experiencing the same thing.

Finally, Lord, I am so thankful that when I call on You Who are without partiality, that You judge according to each one's work. I will conduct myself throughout my time here in fear and reverence. Lord, I will not become so casual, and even presumptuous, with You that I forget to honor and glorify You. I know that I was not redeemed with corruptible things, like silver or gold, or by aimless and meaningless conduct received by tradition from my ancestors, but with the precious blood of Jesus Christ, as of a Lamb without blemish and without spot. All glory and honor be Yours. I pray in Jesus' name. Amen.

CHAPTER 9

THE ANTIDOTE TO SUICIDE AND

SUICIDAL THOUGHTS:

FROM SUFFERING TO GLORY

1 Peter 1:20-21

He indeed was foreordained before the foundation of the world but was manifest in these last times for you who through Him believe in God, who raised Him from the dead and gave Him glory, so that your faith and hope are in God.

****

He indeed was foreordained before the

foundation of the world,

This simply means that God had already planned how to save the world and mankind before there was ever a need for salvation. You see, as the all-knowing One, God knew man would choose sin and be lost to Him forever, unless He did something.

but was manifest in these last times for you ²¹ *who through Him believe in God,*

That "something" was in providing Someone to be the One He would use to solve the problem before Him. He needed Someone to redeem, or buy back, His family. He needed a Man through Whom He would make all men new again in spirit, then at the end of time, in body, all because we believed in, and were brought back to God, through Christ's sacrificial death on the Cross.

who raised Him from the dead and gave Him glory

Why do we have this hope? Because after Jesus died on the cross He was indeed resurrected from the dead, so that we who were *dead* in sin and in our spirit, one of the eternal parts of our being, would live again. As we have seen numerous times in this book and as we have all experienced in this life, there is suffering in the world. Jesus also suffered, died, and was resurrected and taken into glory after He was glorified.

so that your faith and hope are in God

Again, our faith in Jesus is possible because of what Jesus did to make possible that relationship with God. He made the way so that we *always* have hope in God — always. Why can we hope at all times and forever? Because God is eternal, and these truths are spiritual as God is spirit. They are not explainable for the most part, but rather, they are to be experienced and exercised in our everyday lives.

PRAYER FROM OPENING SCRIPTURE

Father God, thank you for Jesus Who was foreordained before the foundation of the world, but was manifest in these last days for us who through Him believe in God, Who raised Him from the dead so that I do not have to die for my sins. I have died and been resurrected just as Jesus was for which You have given Him glory, so that my faith and hope are in You, Oh God. Thank you, Lord, for this victory I have in Jesus Christ. I am a victor over all the works of the enemy and even my own sin because of His sacrifice to make me Your child. I praise Him, and I honor and glorify You, in the Name of Jesus Christ. Amen.

CHAPTER 10

SATAN TOSSED OUT OF HEAVEN &

DEFEATED AT THE CROSS

The Bible tells us that Satan roams around "as" a roaring lion." [1 Peter 5:8] It does not say he *is,* but he *as* a master deceiver is able to produce the effects of more power than he has. Make no mistake — he does have power; but he is no match for the Lion of Judah. The verse goes on to say that Satan is seeking whom he might devour or consume. Suicide is a giving over your life and allowing the enemy to consume it. That's why the armor and offensive weapons are necessary.

We also know that Satan, once called Lucifer, the most beautiful archangel, became so filled with pride that he wanted to usurp God's position and ascend to God's throne. Many know that he started a rebellion in heaven in which one third of the angels fought on his side against God and the other two thirds of the angels. Although this was a war in heaven, Lucifer's power was no match for God's. He was summarily kicked out of heaven down to the earth, where he is now in the spiritual and invisible dimension. So, we may not see him, but we see the effects of his dark kingdom. [Revelation 12:7; Luke   10:18]

So why are we speaking about Satan? Because he is the one behind suicide and all such death and destruction. Anything that has to do with darkness and maleficence can be attributed to the devil.

In the Scripture citation below, Jesus had sent out the 72 witnesses to do the work of the Kingdom: casting out demons, unclean spirits from people, healing the sick, cleansing the leper, and raising the dead. When they were reporting back to Jesus, they were excitedly relating to Him how even the demons were subject to them. He set them straight about their enthusiasm about having power over demons:

Luke 10:17-20

17 Then the seventy returned with joy, saying, "Lord, even the demons are subject to us in Your Name."

18 And He said to them, "I saw Satan fall like lightning from heaven. 19 Behold, I give you the authority to trample on serpents and scorpions, and over all the power of the enemy, and nothing shall by any means hurt you. 20 Nevertheless do not rejoice in this, that the spirits are subject to you, but rather rejoice because your names are written in heaven."

I must admit something. We tend to call any kind of struggle with the demonic kingdom spiritual "warfare". But isn't it interesting that in Ephesians 6, Paul refers to it as a "wrestle." Friend, there is a huge difference between a *war* and a *wrestle*. We know that wars can go on for years, but a wrestle is usually for a pretty short time (except perhaps when Jacob wrestled with the Angel of the Lord, which lasted all night). [Genesis 32: 22-31] So, my point is we do ourselves an injustice by *always* revering the wrestle as a war. Sometimes, we are only experiencing a wrestle, and it will pass. Jesus has already won the war for our souls.

That reminds me of when the 12 spies came back from the land of Canaan: 10 reported "the giants are too big, and we cannot take them." [Numbers 13 and 14 for full account] Two, Joshua and Caleb, came back and said, essentially, "They ain't nothin'. We can take'em. No biggie." What a change in perspective. Guess which of these God honored? He honored the ones who trusted in Him.

This brings me to the "giants" you and I face. First of all, no giant is bigger than God. Remember, he led a young man to slay a giant who had a huge sword, and what did the young man use? He used only one smooth stone. A stone. Now how many people pitting a stone against a sword would think the stone would win? This tells me that with God in the equation, it does not matter what weapon the enemy has. My God says in Isaiah 54:17 that "no weapon formed against me will prosper."

What or whom do we have to fear, but God? God is almighty! No other person, power, or entity can compare to Him in power. If you are a child of God, you have nothing to fear. Your greatest challenge or biggest giant is absolutely no match for Him. So, let's jump into the previously referenced passage of Scripture from Luke in which we read of the 72 witnesses who came back with their reports of vanquishing demons in the name of Jesus. [Luke 10:17-20]. It is clear that it was not something they labored at. I believe they were shocked at how easy it was. I believe we can learn from this. We make this huge deal about wars — and I don't doubt that some do exist — but Jesus did not teach us to make careers out of warring with demons, but rather, to make quick work of the momentary wrestle.

Jesus told them not to get excited about the fact that the demons were subject to them in His Name. He said not to focus on that, even though the authority He had given them was much greater than they thought. No, He told them to focus on the fact that their names were written in heaven. Isn't that surprising? Who would not be excited about having great victories over the enemy? But do you see how quickly a person can descend into pride because of that? Who is the master of pride? Satan is. That is why Jesus mentioned that Satan has fallen. His pride had caused him to challenge God even to the point of "warring" for God's position in God's heaven. Astounding! Jesus was essentially saying, "Satan has already lost, and I saw the fall when he fell from heaven. So, don't make such a big deal about what you have been able to do."

What does that mean for us? Satan is already defeated. He was able to convince one third of the angels to join in his rebellion against God; they warred in heaven and were summarily tossed out. Where were they tossed to? Right here on earth! That is why we on the earth are attacked by the enemy. He hated God and warred against Him. He lost that war so now he wars against God's people — His sons and daughters. That's you and I, who have chosen to follow Christ. There is nothing that the devil can do that changes his position or ours. He has lost. Do not give in to the lie that you have been overcome. Jesus in John 16:33 tells us that we are going to have trouble in this world; but Jesus has overcome the world, and as we remain in Him, we overcome the world and the devil who has been tossed down here. God be praised!

You have already overcome!

PRAYER FROM OPENING SCRIPTURE

Dear Lord, thank you for my life and that I may have Your joy in it. Help me to remember that the demons are subject to me in Your Name and that their master, Satan, was thrown down out of heaven. Oh, Lord, I had forgotten that You gave us authority to trample on serpents and scorpions and over all the power of the enemy and that nothing can hurt me. But of all these things, my greatest joy is in knowing that my name is written in heaven where I will live with you for the rest of eternity. Lord, I see now how my current situation is only temporary but that my joy in You is forever.

CHAPTER 11

IDENTITY IN CHRIST

I could not complete a book directed at preventing suicide and suicidal thoughts without addressing the crucial issue of identity in Christ and functioning in the Spirit. To do so succinctly, I could think of no better Scripture than Romans 8. This tells us about walking in the Spirit even though we are flesh. For the believer in Jesus Christ, Who Himself became flesh, being of physical flesh does not equate to functioning in a fleshly and worldly manner. We may be externally flesh but we ought not to be that way on the inside, that is, in our invisible life such as our thoughts and our personality. We are to function as redeemed ones. Let's get into what it means to say our identity is in Christ instead of in the flesh and in and of this world system.

We will touch on Romans 8, from verses 1 through 30. I will be paraphrasing so that this can be more "conversational." However, please carefully read the Scriptures on your own with the help of the Holy Spirit, our ultimate Teacher, Helper, and Counselor. And a good concordance is always a helpful companion when studying the Scriptures. That said, let's get into it.

Romans 8:1-30

Free from Indwelling Sin

There is therefore now no condemnation to those who are in Christ Jesus, who do not walk according to the flesh, but according to the Spirit. ² For the law of the Spirit of life in Christ Jesus has made me free from the law of sin and death. ³ For what the law could not do in that it was weak through the flesh, God did by sending His own Son in the likeness of sinful flesh, on account of sin: He condemned sin in the flesh, ⁴ that the righteous requirement of the law might be fulfilled in us who do not walk according to the flesh but according to the Spirit. ⁵ For those who live according to the flesh set their minds on the things of the flesh, but those who live according to the Spirit, the things of the Spirit. ⁶ For to be carnally minded is death, but to be spiritually minded is life and peace. ⁷ Because the [c]carnal mind is enmity against God; for it is not subject to the law of God, nor indeed can be. ⁸ So then, those who are in the flesh cannot please God.

Summarizing what this portion of Scripture is telling us, those who are *in* Christ, enabled by the Holy Spirit to follow in His footsteps, are not condemned. We who follow are not under the law because we follow the One Who is the very embodiment and fulfillment of the Law. As we follow the One Who has fulfilled the Law, so we too fulfill the law. You cannot be under something of which you are the fulfillments. So, there is the freedom *from* the Law in a sense, whereas people who are fleshly with the minds on the things of the flesh can never please God nor accomplish the things of God. The fleshly person is focused on that which the world brings. But we who are of the Spirit with our minds on the things of the Spirit are more focused on that which brings life and peace.

This tells us that when we are in the Spirit, our fruit will be life and peace. Death only is produced by the flesh and fleshly thinking. We all are still in these bodies of flesh, but the flesh that is described here is not about the physical body but about the focus of our lives. What determines how we live — the natural things or those of the

Spirit? What concerns us? Who orders our lives? Do we, or do we have a lord who does this? Well, we all have a lord, whether it be self, the enemy of our souls, or the Lord God Almighty.

I submit that it is not difficult to focus on and follow the Lord. The difficulty is in giving up our own rights to determine what we do, where we go, what the focus on, what we say, and so on. Once we have come to a place of submission where we give up all rights to ourselves, we are set. But guess what? We must do this on a daily basis. We have to daily "deny ourselves, take up our cross(es) and follow Him." [Luke 9:23] We must daily crucify the flesh because it wants its own way. We must daily take on the mind of Christ. We must daily be of this mind that was also in Christ. Philippians 2:5-11 tell us this:

> [5] Let this mind be in you which was also in Christ Jesus, [6] who, being in the form of God, did not consider it [b]robbery to be equal with God, [7] but [made Himself of no reputation, taking the form of a bondservant, *and* coming in the likeness of men. [8] And being found in appearance as a man, He humbled Himself and became obedient to *the point of* death, even the death of the cross. [9] Therefore God also has highly exalted Him and given Him the name which is above every name, [10] that at the name of Jesus every knee should bow, of those in heaven, and of those on earth, and of those under the earth, [11] and *that* every tongue should confess that Jesus Christ *is* Lord, to the glory of God the Father.

It takes humility to realize that we do not have it all figured out, that we cannot live this life on our own without God, and that we must intentionally engage Him at all stages of our lives. This life is tough. Anyone who says otherwise is living in a dream world. However, anything that threatens to overcome you, Christ has already overcome. Hence, being *in* Him is essential to walking in the victory He won for us on Calvary.

Twice, that I recall, we learn that we cannot please God: here in Romans 1:8, by being in the flesh, and in Hebrew 11:6, if we have no faith. Why? Because the works of the flesh are death and destruction, and without works, our faith is dead. In both cases, there is death. So, we much walk according to the Spirit of God and we must have faith. Actually, it is impossible to have faith unless we are in the Spirit.

VICTORY OVER THE FLESH AS WE

LIVE IN THE SPIRIT

Romans 8:9-11:

[9] But you are not in the flesh but in the Spirit, if indeed the Spirit of God dwells in you. Now if anyone does not have the Spirit of Christ, he is not His. [10] And if Christ is in you, the body is dead because of sin, but the Spirit is life because of righteousness. [11] But if the Spirit of Him who raised Jesus from the dead dwells in you, He who raised Christ from the dead will also give life to your mortal bodies through His Spirit who dwells in you.

Paul then tells people how they can know that they are not in the flesh but in the Spirit: it is when the Spirit of God dwells in them. And if they are in Christ they are dead to sin because of the righteousness of Christ. We are made righteous, placed in right standing with God, through Christ's sacrificial act on the Cross of Calvary. But this is so important because we are speaking of suicide and suicidal thoughts. With the Spirit of God living in us we are not overcome by thoughts of death and suicide because that same Spirit was responsible for raising Jesus from death *to* life, not death *from* life. God's Spirit never causes death from life. Therefore, that same Spirit of God, the Almighty One, can never be overcome by death and neither can anyone in whom the Spirit abides. The Spirit of God gives life through His indwelling in us. And here Paul is speaking not just about the spiritual life that we get from the Spirit of God; He is referring specifically to verse 11 of Romans 8 to life to the mortal body, that is the physical being. Lest we think this is all spiritual manifestation, Paul tells us that the mortal, physical body is given life through the Spirit of God.

Why is this so important? The Bible is ever consistent; that is why we can believe in it 100 percent. Keep in mind that when God created man in the Garden of Eden, man was only a pile of flesh, well-formed though he was, but just a pile of flesh and bones — that is until the Spirit of God *breathed* His life into man. Listen! Not only are we made in the image of God, *we carry a physical, though unseen part of Him; we have His breath!* Let that sink in for a moment. Death has no place until God says it is time to leave this physical body behind to come to Him in the next phase of our eternal life. You do not want to choose when that time is. God alone reserves that right. God alone appoints that time. [Ecc. 3:2; Heb. 9:27].

Sonship Through the Spirit

12 Therefore, brethren, we are debtors—not to the flesh, to live according to the flesh. 13 For if you live according to the flesh you will die; but if by the Spirit you put to death the deeds of the body, you will live. 14 For as many as are led by the Spirit of God, these are sons of God. 15 For you did not receive the spirit of bondage again to fear, but you received the Spirit of adoption by whom we cry out, "Abba, Father." 16 The Spirit Himself bears witness with our spirit that we are children of God, 17 and if children, then heirs—heirs of God and joint heirs with Christ, if indeed we suffer with Him, that we may also be glorified together.

Paul then exhorts the Corinthians, and now us, that living according to the flesh will cause death. The conclusion: we have descended into fleshly thinking when suicidal thoughts are entertained in our minds. We cannot be blamed for a thought that comes from the evil one but entertaining it and allowing it to make a home in our minds will only cause more morbidity and perhaps the final fruit of suicide. The key is to never entertain a suicidal thought.

75

If it comes, pull down that thought because it is competing against your faith and life in Christ.

When you are living according to the Spirit, you are not going to entertain those thoughts of death that are sent by the thief. You must put those thoughts to death. Those thoughts are not only fleshly, they bring death; so, for a son or daughter of God living according to the Spirit of God, those things have no place because they bring bondage to fear. Fear is a main reason people commit suicide; they are fearful of some circumstance or event that they do not think God can help them through. That's a fleshly thought and it has no place. It must be pulled down.

Paul continues to write that God did not give us a bondage to fear, but we have the Spirit of adoption to at any time cry out, "Abba Father." In those times of despair, we must cry out, "Abba Father." He will never ignore the cry of a son or daughter — never. Listen, not only are we the children of God who live by His Spirit, we are co-heirs with Jesus Christ. That's significant! Think of what it means to be just as entitled as Jesus Christ to the Father's goods and His great name!! But guess what! Just as Christ suffered, so do we get to suffer that we, as Jesus did, may receive glory after our suffering. However, let's remember that God is not the original source of our suffering, suffering, rather, is a manifestation of the fallen world, or a result of our own actions, failures to act, or the actions of others.

I am in no way minimizing the suffering of others. God knows I have known my own suffering and will again; that is how it is to live in this current dispensation of life on earth. But this suffering is only for a very short time compared to eternity. And the best parts of this suffering are that 1) Jesus suffered first and more significantly than we do, and (the best part) 2) we do not suffer alone. He promises to never leave us nor forsake us. That is huge and therein lies our hope. His name is Jesus and absolutely nothing is impossible for Him.

Romans 8:18-25

From Suffering to Glory

¹⁸ For I consider that the sufferings of this present time are not worthy to be compared with the glory which shall be revealed in us. ¹⁹ For the earnest expectation of the creation eagerly waits for the revealing of the sons of God. ²⁰ For the creation was subjected to futility, not willingly, but because of Him who subjected it in hope; ²¹ because the creation itself also will be delivered from the bondage of ^[i]corruption into the glorious liberty of the children of God. ²² For we know that the whole creation groans and labors with birth pangs together until now. ²³ Not only that, but we also who have the first fruits of the Spirit, even we ourselves groan within ourselves, eagerly waiting for the adoption, the redemption of our body. ²⁴ For we were saved in this hope, but hope that is seen is not hope; for why does one still hope for what he sees? ²⁵ But if we hope for what we do not see, we eagerly wait for it with perseverance.

Here, Paul is saying that our current suffering, no matter how bad it may seem and if we persist in walking with the Lord, pales in comparison to the coming glory He will reveal *in* us. Our suffering is temporary, and it is worth it once we see what is to come.

And this is one of my most favorite chapters in Scripture because it tells us what is really happening as we suffer and how God is glorified as we remain steadfast. It says the creation is groaning and waiting for the true sons and daughters of God to be revealed. He is saying that the creation itself was given over to waste but that there is this glorious hope in Christ who will free it from its current bondage of corruption as we, God's adopted children, walk out our purpose of demonstrating the Kingdom of God. We are the ones to bring liberty to all creation as we follow the ultimate Liberator Jesus Christ. Our suffering means we are all subject to and experiencing the birth pangs of the Creation as created ones ourselves. But we know from our high-school biology classes that the birthing process is temporary and compared to all of life it is short.

Our *birth pangs* cause us to groan within ourselves as we await the fulfillment of His adoption and redemption of these physical bodies for immortal ones. All physical ailments, and those of the soul, will be a thing of the past when we see Him. That is the hope we were saved into and still await, but *we must persevere.* We simply must.

WE ARE TOLD TO OVERCOME AND ENDURE TO THE END

The Lord said in Hebrews 10:38-39, that "I take no pleasure in those who put their hands to the plow and draw back." Hebrews 10:38 tells us (this is so good!), *"Now the just shall live by faith; but if anyone draws back My soul has no pleasure in him."* In other portions of Scripture, He tells us that we must hold on to the end, especially in Matthew 24:13 where we read, "But he who endures till the end shall be saved." Instead of the word "saved" some translations say "delivered."

And in Revelation, Jesus gives special promises to those who overcome. In Revelation 3:12 He says, *"He who overcomes, I will make him a pillar in the temple of My God and he shall go out no more. I will write on him the name of My God and the name of the city of My God, the New Jerusalem, which comes down from out of heaven* from My God, and I will write on him My new name." Then in verse 21 of the same chapter He promises, *"To him who overcomes, I will grant to sit with me on my throne as I also overcame and sat down with My Father on His throne."*

These are incomparable rewards. There are no words to describe and no category in which to place them to help us to understand them fully. Even apart from the opportunity to spend life in Paradise with God forever, these rewards go above and beyond what a person should expect; yet the Lord tells us this is what we can expect if we endure to the end and overcome what threatens to overcome *us*.

Here is the consistency of Scripture. Do you remember in John 16:33 when Jesus said this: *"These things I have spoken to you, that in Me you may have peace. In the world you will have tribulation; but be of good cheer, I have overcome the world."*

WE DO NOT FACE OUR SUFFERING ALONE; WE HAVE AN INTERCESSOR WHO GOES AHEAD OF US

Romans 8:26-27

26 Likewise the Spirit also helps in our weaknesses. For we do not know what we should pray for as we ought, but the Spirit Himself makes intercession [g] for us with groanings which cannot be uttered. 27 Now He who searches the hearts knows what the mind of the Spirit is, because He makes intercession for the saints according to the will of God.

But friends, as I shared before, we are not expected to do this alone. This life is hard, and God knows it and Jesus experienced it. He knows what we are made of and that we need the aid of the Helper. That is why He asked the Father to send us the ultimate Helper in the Holy Spirit. He helps us in our weaknesses, which are many. He intercedes for us with the Father in ways we cannot hear, know, or even utter in our own defense or to help ourselves. He is always doing so. And the best part is we do not even have to know or articulate the problem to God because the Holy Spirit is searching our hearts concerning those things for which we need intercession, all within the will of Almighty God. What have we to fear? Nothing. Whom   have   we   to   fear?   No   one.

NO MATTER WHAT WE FACE, GOD KNOWS, HAS KNOWN, AND USES IT FOR OUR GOOD

TO HIS GLORY

Romans 8:28-30:

28 And we know that all things work together for good to those who love God, to those who are the called according to His purpose. 29 For whom He foreknew, He also predestined to be conformed to the image of His Son, that He might be the firstborn among many brethren. 30 Moreover whom He predestined, these He also called; whom He called, these He also justified; and whom He justified, these He also glorified.

Finally, when it comes to our identity in Christ, we can be assured that whatever we face in this life, God can use it for good. At the time of the suffering, it makes no sense that we should suffer so; and we wonder sometimes if God knows or cares. Rest assured, He does know, and He does care; but as His thoughts and ways are so much higher than ours, we simply cannot understand at the time why and what could be gained by such suffering, that is, until later when we see, in retrospect, how God has used the difficulty we have faced. What else do we see? We see that the difficulty was temporary. Trials always are. And that is the mercy of God in placing mankind *within* while He sits outside of it. He is not constrained by time or space, but we are for our protection and preservation.

Knowing all of our lives before we were even born, God knew our personalities, the challenges we would face and how He would use them to shape us into the image of Jesus Christ, the only One Who has been accepted back into heaven. Therefore, the Jesus-like ones are the ones who will be accepted into heaven to live forever with Him. Believe it or not, our sufferings make us like Jesus if we allow God to use them. After all, Jesus Himself learned obedience by

His suffering. How much more, then, we need to endure through our challenges for God to shape Jesus Christ in us?!

In other words, the God of our suffering — whether that suffering is of our own making or not, and if we submit to Him, repenting where it is warranted and trusting Him as Lord and Savior — will use it to give us that Christ-like character He is looking for in every believer. And in the end, He gets the glory for how He used *all* things for good.

He foreknew that we would become His and predestined those who would make the decision to be His sons and daughters to be conformed to the image of Christ, His First-born. He called us, granting gifts and talents to fulfill the callings, justified us as if we had never sinned, and glorifies us at the appointed time. That is the journey of the child of God with the identity of God as displayed in the Son, and our destination is glory.

The goal of Satan is to cut us off as early as he can from that process. Whenever a person gives up, through suicide or other means such as leaving the faith, he or she falls victim to Satan's schemes to steal, kill, and destroy. This does not have to happen.

I guarantee you this: If you cry out to God in your despair, He will by no means ignore you. He will hear you and send you help. No matter what you do, do not listen to evil counsel to perform that ultimate act of destruction. Know who you are and Whose you are — no less that a son or daughter of Almighty God. And if you are not yet a child of God, do not wait. Seek Him as Lord as Savior today and He will be yours. "A bruised reed He will not break." [Isaiah 42:3; Matthew 12:20] In your weakness, He will neither refuse you nor allow for your destruction.

Be of good cheer; Jesus has overcome the world and so can you.

CHAPTER 12

CONCLUSION

We have built a Biblical foundation for solidly walking through challenges so intense that you or someone you know may have contemplated suicide. Let's summarize what we've covered thus far in a   roadmap to victory over suicide and suicidal thoughts.

ROADMAP TO THE ANTIDOTE for SUICIDE

AND SUICIDAL THOUGHTS

First, we looked at the reasons people make the drastic decision to kill themselves or start thinking in that way. The answer to that is fear of a circumstance and a hopelessness in the possibility of deliverance from that assumed dreadful situation.

Second, we looked at Christians specifically, the purveyors of hope in Jesus Christ, Author of everything for Whom nothing is impossible. The reason this occurs is because there is a temporary or growing lack of faith that God could solve a problem and deliver the individual from a person or situation they fear would happen.

Third, we looked at the spiritual warfare that we face every day and the best defense and offense with which to wage a good warfare and secure your victory in Christ.

Fourth, we discussed the fact that the attacks we face are mainly in our minds. The enemy has determined that if he could beat us on that battlefield, he has us. However, the Word of God tells us how to protect our minds and keep it free from strongholds set up there against belief and faith in God.

Fifth, in the second part of the book, we laid out the various parts of the antidote to suicide, suicidal thoughts and tendencies as laid out in 1 Peter 3, verses 1 through 5 and the fact that *we always have hope in life through the resurrection Jesus Christ from death to life*. He was the first born from the dead, which means He died the death for all those who would call upon His name and believe in Him.

Then, sixth, we looked at another component of the antidote to suicide and suicidal thoughts in 1 Peter 1: 6-9, particularly at the fact that in this life we will suffer tribulations, but those sufferings are only temporary, and they are effective in testing our faith in Jesus Christ. Therefore, if we will but hold onto — no, cling to — the Lord, He will always deliver us. Then, and only then, do we have the makings of great testimonies of His deliverance from hard times. Without a test, there can be no testimony to those who are still wondering, "Who is this Jesus and what's the big deal anyway?" and other questions like, "How is the life of Jesus even relevant to my life today?" Your story, your testimony is the key to explaining the reason He is a "big deal" and His relevance to our lives today. Think of it this way: through our temporary suffering, Jesus brings others to glory.

Seventh, we saw the importance of the *alignment between our mind, our thoughts, and our obedience to the Word of God*, in 1 Peter 1:13-16.

Eighth, we saw another component of the antidote to suicide in 1 Peter 1:17-19: *the powerful redemption through the blood of Christ.* Without His shed blood, there is no redemption because there is no death from which He would rise. That death and resurrection seals those who believe for the day of ultimate salvation at His soon coming return to earth.

Ninth, we continued with the antidote to suicide in 1 Peter 1:20-21, that just like Jesus *our temporary suffering leads to glory.* Now "glory" is a word that can be confusing and is not in everyone's vocabulary. If you are a believer in Christ, chances are you know what it means, though that is not necessarily the case. I find that precious few people know what the glory referred to here means. The best way I can think of to break it down is really in the life of Christ and the difference between time and eternity. Anything that happens in time is temporal, seasonal, and will be over at some point. God placed us, His creations, in time because He loves us and because He knows that one day all the trappings and difficulties on this earth in this dispensation of the history of man must come to an end. Otherwise, the death and resurrection of Christ would be for nothing. We would remain in our misery. So, anything in time is temporary. Suffering is in time, so it is always temporary. One day, there would be none of that .... only glory.

Glory is eternal, not inside of time but outside of it. Think of Jesus. After He had suffered death on the cross, He rose again and was on the earth for about 40 days. That's an estimation. After that, the Bible tells us, He was taken up into glory and, at that time, the angel that appeared to the disciples as they were looking up in awe at what had just occurred told them that just as Christ as ascended there from the Mount of Olives, He would return and touch down in the very same way and place in which He left. [Acts 1:11] In this context, glory means heaven or the heavenly realm. It is not part of tangible nature. And for all intents and purposes, it is a place and a state of being in that place. Jesus had to receive His glorified body in order to return to glory, that heavenly realm. But the Bible also tells us that when He appears once again, we will be as He is, glorified. [Romans 8:17-18] Why? Because at that time we will have experienced our suffering and it will be over.

Tenth, in Luke 10:17-20, Jesus described how He saw Satan tossed out of heaven before He utterly defeated him at the Cross.

Then, eleventh, and crucial to all that has been discussed here is *our identity in Christ* as laid out in Romans 8. We see pictures and demonstrations of our identity in Christ all through Scripture. So, I am not limiting us to this passage of the Bible in which we find our identity. However, I find that this Scripture is very effective at bringing home to us in bold and expressive language who we are as spiritual sons and daughters of the King of kings and Lord of lords.

You see, without a good handle on who we are in Christ, we can become susceptible to believe any lie Satan throws at us. And these tactics are as old as the world is, starting even in the Garden of Eden. The devil was able to tempt the first couple to sin because they temporarily forgot who they were. They were already *like* God, yet the devil got them to doubt it and fall into sin, which they immediately regretted because they began to lose parts of their God-likeness; for instance, death entered in. They were never created to die yet based on the warning issued to them about eating from that particular tree, death was essentially "born".

My friend, we have come to the end of this book. I pray, that in these pages and throughout your reading of Scripture, the Lord has demonstrated His love, His commitment, and your new identity to you. You have been bought with a price, redeemed from death to an abundant life. That is regardless of how you feel at the moment. We know that feelings come and go, but God is the same yesterday, today, and forever. He never changes, and He never leaves us physically nor forsakes us emotionally or mentally. He is always right there and accessible. Never accept the lies of the enemy that God is not there for you. He is and always will be. He is trustworthy. He loved us first even when we had no thought of Him and *were* dead in our sins. There is no more death to die. It's done. Live in His love. Cry out to Him in your need and worship and praise Him in the midst of your challenges; then, see how long those challenges, no matter how difficult, can stay. They end up being quite short-lived. He is for you and not against you. [Jer. 29:11-13; Rom.8:31].

Now, may He bless you on your journey and firmly establish you as one who would testify of His goodness in hard times. Glory to the One Who has taken you out of darkness and has placed you in the Kingdom of light.

ABOUT THE AUTHOR

Auriol Sonia Morris, JD is a multi-level communicator and minister of the Truth. She has been a missionary business teacher at a Chinese university, where she developed her love for teaching. She especially enjoys teaching from God's Word.   Ms. Morris is a creative solutionist by God's grace and enjoys seeing lives transformed by His Truth. Having earned law and master's in government degrees, she has worked in practically every arena of society from financial services to legal and everything in-between. Through worldwide travel, God has placed her in many different spheres among many different kinds of people. She loves to travel and would welcome the opportunity to share from any of her books or any other area of Bible-based Kingdom reality.

[i] John 14:30; Matt/ 16:23, "Get thee, behind me, Satan, you are not mindful of the things of God but the things of the world."

[ii] John 14:27.

[iii] He is bringing His reward with Him. Rev. 22:12.

[iv] I Corinthians 9:27.

[v] Luke 9:35; John 14:26; John 16:13; 1 Corinthians 2:10.

[vi] John 15:5.

[vii] Luke 1:37.

[viii] 2 Timothy 1:7.